A Story of One

A STORY OF

One

Transcen*Dance*

GRACE GABRIELLA PUSKAS

2020
GOLDEN DRAGONFLY PRESS

FIRST PRINT EDITION, December 2020
FIRST EBOOK EDITION, December 2020

Copyright © 2020 by Grace Gabriella Puskas
Cover art and interior art © 2020 by Alina Gaboran.

ISBN: 978-1-7325772-7-5

Library of Congress Control Number: 2019937594

Printed on acid-free paper supplied by a
Forest Stewardship Council-certified provider.
First published in the United States of America
by Golden Dragonfly Press, 2020.

www.goldendragonflypress.com

*There is a new blueprint waiting to be birthed, it begins with a shift
in frequency, there are many different timelines here to choose
for our best reality.*

*We can live up to destiny and we can remember who we truly are,
for our souls carry the unique vibration which we brought
from another star.*

*We choose our timeline, we choose our fate, the doorways
to transcend are always in play.*

*We can stay stuck in our spirals, we can continue to devolve,
or we can embrace our immortality in a way that's pure Gold.*

A Story of One: Transcendance is a poetic love story of music, telepathy and purity, a mystical poetic rendition of the Magi Mind. It is a transcendental tantric dance of the senses birthing a new vibration for planet earth and the best possible reality for Gaia herself.

Contents

A Story of Creation

The apple:
it gets a bite taken,
a part of his being absorbed into the flesh
of this man, this forsaken—
devil?

The earthly form:
it merges with this creature's soul
allowing his divinity to be diluted
to the physical world.

A sin?

The light
of this spiritual creature
becomes tainted with darkness,
the shadow—a teacher;
the punishment?

The snake:
he observes the scene,
witness to the wisdom gifted,
the duality of being imprisoned whilst free…
A curse—

or a blessing?

The tree—
the snake's home,
the creator of the apple
and life giver of breath to man's soul—
the culprit?

The moon…
she is a silent yet powerful witness,
her subconscious that allows
all the interacting parts their existence.

Is she evil?

The sun—
he is the energy for the picture below,
the destructive force
that paradoxically allows growth.

God?

Spirit,
flowing through all that is,
neither masculine nor feminine
but a combined state of bliss.

Do we fear this?

Oneness...
How shall we separate this?

Matters of the Mind

I know when you think about me,
I can feel you at my core—
no matter how hard I try to be free I can block you out no more.

You project a wave which radiates through space,
I can feel your energy from any distant place.
Your emotion is so intense—
it becomes absorbed through my lens
and my aura receives,
leaving my mind to perceive
what this all means?

My sensitivity to external influence
and my ability to sense
your thought projections
from so far away…

yet is it all just a reflection?
Are these feelings mine or yours,
is it all in my mind, all crazy talk?
How can I possibly comprehend what is real
when reality itself is an illusion,
all the different parts creating this holistic confusion.

You and I—I and you,
yes—there are two
but then why does it feel like we are one?
If all that exists between us is space
and this space is connected, atom to atom,
so each atom creates an interweaving interaction
and there really is no such thing as us existing as two,
how do I know if these feelings belong to me or to you?

Does it even matter?

Matter—
what an ironic choice of word.
Matter is just energy,
an energetic vibration existing as a certain frequency;
atoms and particles vibrating at different speeds,
the matter in question subject to what my mind perceives.

What I create to be true is what my mind believes
and we all know the mind can deceive,
so, once again, is this you or me?

Now it does not matter, the thought has passed.

I remembered to breathe.

The Beginning of the End

It's dark. No sunshine illuminates the walls,
I see colours bouncing and dancing,
the unconscious becomes lighted from source,
a memory long lost surfacing.

I have been here before,
in another time.
Wisdom becomes absorbed
from the spaces in between—my mind,
floating timelessly around.

I breathe in deeply;
hearing my heartbeat echoing around me,
green... red... gold...
swirling energetically.
I have definitely been here,
in this moment, in this now.

Time disappears into a timeless reality
as I merge into the inner bliss of eternity.

The End of the Beginning

I start to feel my flesh tingling,
my form becoming a provider for nature's feeding.
The acoustic vibrations of these creatures disrupt my heaven,
bring my awareness back to my earthly vessel;
and the more I focus on the surrounding sounds,
the echoes—the buzzing,
the drip… drip… drip of rainwater and my blood pumping—

I remember.

I am in a beautiful mountain Buddhist Vipassana
with birds singing and trees swaying for my security,
and a body to nurture me spirit-u-ally.
This is why I separated from God, from Source,
I wanted to *feel*—to sense,
to learn and grow through a human lens.

A part of me would love to stay in that cave
meditate every day
and feel that oneness;
but this world is calling me.

So when I am far away
and when the immortality is craved,
the memory remains.
I know now to look within,
as that feeling didn't emanate from that cave in Mae Hong Son,
it was inside my skin.

Now my journey begins.

Walk-In Wanderer

They think they know her, they think, they *think*,
but mind is only one aspect, in just one blink—
the whole universe changes, who is looking through these eyes;
who is looking through these eyes and who is speaking through this
    mind?
They think they see her, but who is she—
which life form is she embodying from an invisible world?
Water cleanses—water purifies,
water is the seed of the soul where memory lies.

The sacred vessel—a conduit,
waiting to be filled with the consciousness of the human monument.
The body is the spiral, the channel transmits and receives,
interconnected to the higher avatar from other galaxies.

The body is the spiral—the channel transmits and receives,
interconnected to the higher avatar from other galaxies.

Earth; one beautiful little planet,
circling round in one solar system inside its own enchantment;
inside just one galaxy—one world,
circling within a greater system to the interconnected whole.

The cells inside the vessel, the cells inside the swirl,
the spiral of the consciousness linked into the interdimensional twirl.
Source particles are in space, they exist in another plane,
source particles are inside the skin of a walk-in wanderer's brain.

Source particles are in space, they exist in another plane,
Source particles are inside the skin of a walk-in wanderer's brain.

Butterfly

The butterfly sang, sweetly in tune,
she knew how to birth the most sensational grooves.
She sang from the heart, she played from the ether,
the most delicate design created by nature.

The butterfly was a beauty, intrinsically designed,
she was created from colours and alchemised from the divine.
Each note attuned, each tone, perfected
celestially put to earth to bring through higher perspectives.

And the girl who didn't care for all those superficial things,
the material accumulations and greed that prevented her sing,
sat silently in her room, birthing sweet sounds—
a young naive girl waiting patiently in her Crown.

Then one day the strings snapped, they broke completely from the core,
the next month the wires came out; they were connected no more;
the colours of the canvas slowly began to crack,
the missing strings resulting in broken songs seeping through the gaps.

The butterfly was her companion, her one and truest friend,
her foundation and root that would love her until the end.
She was real—true—and beautifully pure,
but in a heartbeat, she became broken and her lifelong friend sang
    no more.

And she could not understand it, sitting peacefully in her room,
how the beauty that once birthed sweet sounds no longer sang
    celestially in tune.
Why did she fall apart, what made her suddenly break—
when the butterfly was the one thing she gave all her trust and faith?

Now the beautiful butterfly sits alone in a dark space,
unloved and abandoned—broke from the core—treated with disgrace.
Perhaps one day the girl will return to the dark and empty place,
and mend this broken instrument with a smile across her face.

And in that time she will be given new strings, created from a newer time,
the electrics will be re-wired—created from a better mind;
the cracks on canvas will be re-filled with colours to match her wholeness,
and the broken beauty—so innocent and loving—will be restored
     back to her golden pureness.

Yet even among the years of neglect, of abandon and incompleteness,
the young girl still maintained her faith, her love, her trust and sweetness;
and although her soulful butterfly companion was lost to lesser things,
the one thing that never, ever broke, was her beautiful butterfly wings.

The Violin with the Green Aura

She breathed in, pure energy trickling up her spine,
she locked eyes with her soul's reflection, pure light radiating
    through her eyes.
She had become a channel, a conduit for light and healing,
a crystal grid connected symbolised by purity and feeling.

DMT activated, she was breathing through another,
the discomfort he felt through releasing all fear being transmuted by
    this earth mother.
She was raising his vibration simply through her light,
her vessel filled with pure source energy, crystallized particles as her sight.

Her inner and outer worlds became one and the same,
she could feel herself outside herself—she no longer had a brain;
her mind became pure consciousness, pure consciousness creating form,
she had transcended all possible limitations of an illusionary
    physical world.

She closed her eyes and went within, a journey into herself,
every particle became an atom, her being absorbed with her soul's cells.
She saw herself as an instrument, the frequency of herself in
    energetic form,
the shape of her formless spirit manifested into the human world.

She was a violin with a green aura floating timelessly in space,
she had become an octave higher of the lower dimensional Grace.
The shift in frequency was real—she knew she was a musical note,
yet what she didn't know at the time was that her cord would change
    the world.

Venus & Mars

Venus, the planet of love and beauty,
bringer of peace, balance and tranquillity.
She is the divine lover, the mother of all planets,
sensuality and grace oozing from her magnetics.

Her auric field is one of calm, caring and warmth,
and her subtle vibrations show you that her love can endure.
For she is purity—the goddess of love and intimacy,
sensuality in its element of all forms of divinity.

Venus is a planet, a goddess and a soul,
a divine incarnation of a vision for our world.
She is gentleness defined by her intentions and enchantment
an entity of love and divine sexuality in embodiment.

Sensuality, romance, purity and passion
are ruled by her as a symbol of love and devotion.
Art, music, nature and all things of beauty
come under Venus' realm with a warmth that is healing energy.

She—the complete opposite of Mars,
sits gracefully in her place amongst the planets and stars.
And she does not wish to take but instead freely gives,
a helper and healer, she creates—she is a gift.

❈　❈　❈

Mars, the planet of war and destruction,
he is the warrior with a strong sense of aggression.
He is the yang to Venus' yin,
a planet of sexuality, action and will.

Mars is primitive, an initiatory force,
he is often quick-tempered with a nature like war.
Impatience, anger, passion and lust
are ruled by this dual planet of sexuality and love.

He is Venus' counterpart, her duality in wholeness,
two faces to the symbol of passion and boldness.
For Mars strives for what he wants with dominance,
active yet forceful with a character of perseverance.

Mars is the inner burning inside of us all,
the lust, need and destruction which can also endure,
for he is competitive, insensitive and aggressive in his ways
desire replacing purity and other beautiful affection displays.

Whilst Mars takes—Venus gives,
whilst Mars lusts, the goddess of love stays in bliss.
When the planet of war wishes only to serve destruction,
the planet of beauty is here to re-mind us of our co-creation.

Her-Story/ Her Twin's HiStory
(Uni-Versal)

He could have had it all, yet he still didn't fully see,
a mind drenched in ego replacing his true destiny.
He lost her the moment he chose lust—
he lost her the moment he chose both of us,
yet she couldn't stand for that, she had her own self-respect
and now her light shines, there's no space for regret.
The moment he chose two, she became one,
her gifts fully free to shine—her song is sung
for his lack of love has allowed her to be,
she is music—she is real—she can now be all she was meant to be.

So she thanks him despite all the years of pain,
despite all the years of being trapped in his game
for if he didn't love many whilst he was still loving her,
she wouldn't be able to rule the world.
And that is what she is doing—and he knows
yet it's too late for him, but he still grows;
and maybe in another life, his soul will choose a path with higher eyes
and the fire-breathing dragon will finally stop causing havoc through
    the streets and skies.
For this timeline is still in play—the destruction,
his soul split in two in both dimensions.
Yet we both know how the story ends, this beautiful symphony
he will live his lie and she will play out her own destiny.
For she has accepted her duality within—yet he needs another,
the woman giving birth and being the life holder.
Maybe one day she might take him back
when her light once again needs the black,
but perhaps it is too late in this life;
he lost it, he blew it—back to mortal life.

He sees—truly—for before she could not speak these words,
rooted in guilt and self-blame with no desire to hurt
as the truth is soul destroying—it really is the saddest story;
but she has cried many tears and now deserves her glory.
She gave him the world, she tried to make him see,
she sacrificed her own love and self-worth for another's ego needs…
and he never thanked her, he never said a single word,
the silence became illusion and the truth remained unheard.
Yet he still dreams of her—he can never let her go fully,
they came to this life together, two twins in a shared story.
But the dragon remains, fuelled with lust, greed and desire,
and he stays trapped in his spiral until he embraces something higher
yet he can't—he won't—not yet in this cycle,
before she was the victim yet now she sees her power.
For years she was testing him, waiting for his word,
and for years he messed around, chaos being all he served.
So she flies solo now, gracefully like a bird,
the only difference being she will never take him back, and this is the
      final word.

Now she is fully free to live her dreams,
him choosing to love more than one being, the Midas touch to her melody;
to her final performance, the masterpiece,
the one with sheer strength and endurance;
the one that places her above the rest—
the one she was truly happy to share.
He could have had it all but time won't wait anymore,
he is no longer that special someone in her magical world.
She sends him love just as she sends love to the passing bird,
her beauty and magic free to shine, her soul to serve
yet in no more darkness or sacrifice—
she is now the star of her own life!
Sometimes he wishes he could join her on her magical ride,
if only he had waited and honoured her pride;
the glory that could have been his for the rest of his days,
he would have shone brighter than any king lost in the maze.
She would have placed him at the top of her celestial mountain,
all who spoke of their love would have seen godly devotion.

They would have travelled around the world as the stars they truly are,
and everyone would know their names, wide and far...

But now she uses her own light to shoot like a star,
and he fuels off his darkness to heal his own heart.
She finds peace in the celestial, the higher and ether,
and he finds comfort in the mundane, maintaining his secret.
She was so lost and confused for so long,
stuck in sadness and the shadow whilst he shone.
But he took her light—he fed off her,
using her love which she still had whilst shamelessly bleeding her.
And each night he would lay next to another,
knowing his selfish ways were keeping her;
stuck, blocked—fully from shining,
he accepted her love whilst subconsciously keeping her in hiding.
Yet he didn't want only her—he just wanted to play,
she felt it all astrally and became stuck in her daze.
He even went as far as denying her new love,
each chance she had for happiness he prevented with a magic touch.
For years he got to have both, even if energetically,
rooted in selfishness, ego and greed.
So she would spend each night alone suffering quietly in silence,
confused and in the shadow realms due to his intended misguidance,
for he would always show her moments of real love in perfect timing,
his manipulation a block which prevented her from shining.
The king she found and grew to love merely became a fantasy,
the delusion of the spun illusion made her feel she was not worthy,
so she clung to his love like a drug keeping her sustained,
his moments of affection and their connection maintained.
And each time she had a chance for real joy, love and peace,
he spun his spell like a wizard—her torture on repeat.

He *thrived* in it—it fuelled his desire,
leaving to go back to chaos instead of transcending to a love that's higher
but she let him, for her love is pure and deep,
her innocence, the shield to the abuse she sustained through sleep.
But she is awake now—she finally sees...
And it is such a sad, sad story;
he could have led his ultimate life if he just wasn't so seedy.

So now she won't repress it—she won't even deny it,
she's living in Gold and harmonizing to the higher.
And as she does this she will keep the real story
and remind him with love how he threw away *real* glory.
Some think she's evil—other's think she's mad,
the truth is she no longer sacrifices or chooses to feel bad
for this is her *swan song*—her final performance,
she has the devotion and strength for a lifetime's endurance.
There's a space open for another now that's no longer him,
a Celestial Crown of jewels and Gold waiting to place upon her King.
One King—and this is her pride,
this is why he will still sometimes cry, even if inside,
because his bittersweet symphony is he knows she is real
it took years of neglect and lies to truly feel—
the truth.

She needed to speak these words, otherwise, she would remain in fear,
remain in regret, blame and false steer;
her life would not be the magic it is without her soul being free
to speak something so pure and true, so poetically.
She could remain to appease him and his chosen wife
and keep herself stuck in the lies and simply hide,
but she did this—for years—whilst they were encompassed in betrayal,
in lust and destruction with no regards to how they kept her enslaved.
And even amongst her soul family, she was forced to dim her light
    to please,
to not live out her true vibration and sacrifice her joy and peace;
for when she shines in her truest form the truth always seeps
    through the cracks,
their betrayal forcing her to leave the soul group she came with, a
    twisted request to never come back.
You can't hide love.

It's real this time—it always has been,
it is said that in a golden Age a King will have many Queens
and one can love more than one wholly and simultaneously,
but she no longer stands for this—she's completely closed his door;
now she flies with her dignity and pride...
Amazing Grace is his no more.

All is love; all is one;
forgiveness is the key to earth's song.

The Story of One has begun.

Mortal Messenger

She could have had all of me—there was nothing more I desired,
she brought out my best and was the one I truly admired.
I loved her, yet she simply played me for a fool,
taking on and off my crown; her favourite game—her private tool.
She loved me yet she couldn't ever show it to make it real,
she enticed me with her purity and harmonised my mind to make me feel.
She was clever in her ways, allowing true emotion and feeling to
    seep through
then like a child who gets bored with her toy she kept leaving to go
    back to school.
Others think she is the best—she really is intelligent,
her soul clearly advanced and her spiritual awareness on a whole
    new level—
yet she would love me and draw me in,
make me believe we could truly win;
then she would simply leave, escape into her own world
thriving in her darkness whilst I was left alone.
And it really is a sad, sad story,
for I could see her sacrifice whilst I experienced my glory.
It would have been her, without a doubt
but she gave up her light and transferred it to black.
How easy it would have been for her to show me how she felt,
the years we could have been sharing love instead of floating in neglect;
in lack of love, in discord,
she gave me her soul but couldn't accept my own world.
I tried to help her see through hybrid eyes,
I had accepted it all yet she maintained her own disguise;
and those moments she could have truly made me her king
she chose to remain in the depths she still swims.
I hear she shines now—gracefully like a bird
and some tell me she still would love to offer me a space in her
    magical world.
Yet it's too late, we had our chance,
her repression, my decision, and her sacrifice my final dance

for I found love, a different type but true,
I've created a world of my own and no longer need her to see me through.
For she is a fool—a beautiful one—but a fool all the same,
she thinks she is the only one who knows how to play the game
and although I do admire her, she really is Amazing Grace,
I came into this world alone and need to play the race at my own pace.

So I thank her and appreciate her for how she made me see,
how she helped me through those years and how she chose to still
    love me.
I respect her and see her for the star she truly is,
but she made her choice and chose her story, going solo was her bliss;
her suppression and lack of touch and affection resulting in me
    following my needs,
each choice I made was with love for myself and to allow me to be free…
You can take a creature to a celestial fountain but you can't make her
    drink the water,
I showed her my love and affection and fully opened my heart for her;
yet she didn't want only me—she played herself at her own game,
no jealousy or grudge as she has evolved higher and no regret or blame,
but with all her magic and all her beauty, all she had to do was to
    transcend with more than words,
then the dragon would no longer be causing destruction, and we'd be
    shining our light all around the world.

All is love; all is one;
forgiveness is the key to earth's song.

The Story of One has begun.

A New Cycle

Just as the seasons come and go,
with each new transit, we are given a chance for growth.
A New Moon represents a beginning—a time for letting go and release
so there is clear space for fresh starts, new birth and opportunity.

A Full Moon marks completion, a cycle coming full swing
where hopefully the lessons have been learnt and integrated,
so they don't come round again.

The illusion is we are separate, distanced from our earth, moon and stars,
yet, in reality, we are One, naturally connected through our hearts.
Like the waves which crash the shore, we have our tides within
tuning in and listening to our rhythms make life truly easier to swim.

Thoughts, emotions, feelings and transits;
our daily life is influenced by the natural world and planets.
When we become aware of the energy currents in play
we can truly master the waves and learn the secrets to the game.

Each month provides us opportunity for healing and release,
for insight, wisdom, and integrations to be complete.
All aspects of our Self wish to be heard,
denying the signs and symbols creating disunity in our world.

Now is the time to listen to the trees, to the earth and to our skies;
for us to hear the waves of the ocean sending signals to our minds.
We are ready to open and receive the moon's ancient wisdom,
embrace our Sun and other planets who are here solely for our existence.
With every energy current, we can connect and journey with nature's
    timeless teachings,
every ending a new beginning, letting go fully and releasing
all that no longer serves so we can create the life we long for,
dreams and visions, intentions and ambitions a reality—our New Path.

So let us now live life in harmony with our essence
for we are nature;
Source in its purest expression.

The Path of the Priestess

She will be your guru; she will be your fire,
she will help you dis-attach and vibrate higher.
She will provide you the space to allow you to be,
no old paradigm illusions polluting divinity.

She knows you—she sees you, you want a love that's true,
that pure unconditional love that reflects the shaman in you.
You want to have fun and you want to be friends,
you want her to view you as a god through her lens.

She will help you dear love, dear brother and lover;
sometimes you will spend time as sister and brother,
allowing the other to remain in their centre
and existing in your freedom and highest potential.
She will stay in her own and never cling to you,
(except for when in bed and you invite her to).
For the rest of the time—she will be your guide,
there will never be jealousy, deceit or false pride
and you will only share through an avatar higher eye.

She will help you dis-attach and vibrate higher
and if she ever feels smothered or her aura violated,
she will tell you there and then with no judgement or hatred.
She will do it in a way that empowers your essence,
bringing it right back to that godly reflection.
She wants you to be the best you—she wants you to be free,
what she doesn't want is for you to start relying on her for all your needs.

The way she perceives you will lead to your greatness,
the energy she projects will empower your status;
your status within—your own sense of Self,
you'll become a magnet and attractive to all you connect.
She will help you see it's ok to feel,
ok to connect and ok to be real.

It is natural for others to get attracted to Source,
your light shining bright, kundalini pure.
She will smile as the opposite sex see you for who you are,
your energy and aura vibrating their hearts.
The natural attraction that others will feel
will be loved and appreciated as she knows that you're real.

She will appreciate and learn from your human imperfections,
all emotions and feelings unconditionally welcome;
and she'll perceive you in a way that will help others shine,
your godliness empowering goddesses to be reflected as divine.

The Priestess is your guide and she is your soul sister
yet when you are alone she will invite you closer.
She will take you to worlds only the mystic knows,
the place to recharge and love light grow.
Your fire and source will burn bright like flames
and she'll show you how to control it for your own inner gain.
You will share and merge on all of the realms,
the heart mind motions and spirit of self.

She will use her Source and centre only to empower,
not taking anything but giving freely as a healer.
Your tantric dance will be watched by the gods,
all eyes from the ether seeing true love.

You will be given the space to be truly free,
no vampire energy to dilute divinity;
nothing will be taken that you don't wish to give,
your energy your own, your freedom—your bliss.
You are the god, you are the fire,
she will make sure that you remain in your centre
and share in true balance—
her tantric lover yes but you're your own independence.
And your etheric dance will end with realization,
your source as duality for individual perception,
the union a way to help us evolve
showing you aspects of self only the priestess knows.
She will share it—freely—you can be her student,

your master, your lover—pure Source in movement.
You will never have to worry about old age illusions,
the old way of being, distortion; confusion,
you will always be respected and treated as an equal;
the way we perceive affects our reality,
our thoughts and projections creating physicality.
She has mastered it all and keeps seeing from the highest,
distancing herself at the right time so you shine the brightest
as she knows that your merging was just a sparking of diamonds.

She will be your guru and she'll be your fire,
she will only have love, support and empower,
and if you ever feel negative emotions from your attachment or oneness
she will make sure in that moment she detaches—independence.

The Priestess will never be hurt as she has realized she is free,
responsible for her own thoughts and emotions, she truly sees.
She is empowered and free and living her own life
and she asks the same from you—no negative vibes.
And if you do treat her in a way that doesn't feel aligned
she will only ever respond with compassion and love,
staying in her centre and remaining in love with love.
She will give you freedom to learn and give you your space,
connected to her own Source, embodying grace.

Divine Encounters

I see all these faces of judgement pierce me down—they frown
whilst I calmly write words of beauty and grace,
there is a smile on my face.

I observe eyes like daggers glare at my clothes,
little do they know I'm writing these words so they can grow.

I wear colourful trousers that—if allowed—can be healing;
yet people perceive me as crazy,
they've simply stopped feeling.
Their minds are over-thinking, believing I'm inferior
because society convinces them their outward appearance is superior.

Their judgement and negativity lead to their despair,
just because nature has given me dread-locked hair.
I continue to write with the hope they will find peace,
wishing one day they can see the heart inside me.

People walking by give me funny looks
because I'm smiling to myself whilst reading a book.
I am absorbed in words of how connected we are,
the philosophy of life expanding my brain and my heart.
I am lost in the magic that literature has to offer
whilst a man in a suit stares down in disdainful wonder.

Strangers look disgusted when I bounce by on a high,
a high received from a smile from a previous passerby.
I am singing to myself, causing no harm and loving life
whilst a metre away I receive eye glances like knives.

When I see a homeless person in the cold on the street,
I show my respect—acknowledge them with a greet.
I sometimes stop to chat and sometimes offer food,
why do people still stare at me so rude?

I've chosen a path which allows me to help others in my community,
I work towards a world of peace, depth, and unity;
I observe others with no judgement and accept them as an equal,
even after all the hate I receive
I still choose to help my people.

I treat others with respect, kindness and support;
I am willing to listen to a stranger in need to talk,
I see everyone for the light that is inside
without any superficial perception
which disconnects us from the divine.

Without any superficial perception,
which disconnects us from the divine.

Magi Minds

He is Krishna, you know;
the way he enters a room and all eyes turn to him,
some inquisitive—others hopeful, most unconsciously intrigued;
the similarity is, they all glow when he speaks.

It's as if he's wearing a cloak of magenta robes,
an ethereal crown of gold laced upon his locks;
his shadow bathed in mystery and appeal,
an air of authority that would match the gods.

If Christ were sent here incarnate
I'm sure he would resemble this entrancing man.
His wisdom is direct—firm yet gentle,
and his lion-like confidence oozes whilst still being humble.

Women admire, there is a soulful longing in their eyes,
a magnetic appeal as sweet as nectar,
a dancing of their cells and tingling of their thighs.
He is Krishna you know.

The subtle vibrations and purity in his thought
ripple out to meet his mirrors,
always committing to oneness and treating all as an equal,
yet he knows, within.

The respect he commands matches that of a king,
a character of harmony, inner balance and clarity,
attractive and glowing in divine physicality,
mind heart and emotions attuned to the highest reality.

He does not abuse his power—oh no,
he channels it wisely to help others grow.
The words he chooses weave golden threads
and his intentions radiate clearly through the interconnected web.

His mind is perfected, everyone knows,
his aura so powerful he stands naked in clothes;
the ancient essence spirals out from within,
the whole frequency of space changes—just from his presence,
like his very being sparks a deep inner remembrance.

This man is God, he's living on another plane,
yet he lives in our world and has evolved to show another way.
Divinity defines him—he reflects it to all he meets,
beauty to perfection, Kingly, he sees.

Tantric Transcendance'

Tantric transcendance, what does it mean?
Is it the embodiment of tantra in a king or a queen?
That primal pulse you feel between your thighs
whilst simultaneously knowing it's coming from your higher eye;
tantric transcendance—it's more real than love,
it's that fire that sparks you without any touch.
The rippling waves of vibration that wash over your skin,
that merging with another without going all in.
Some see it dark, others see the truth,
the knowing that divinely connects one as two.

The fire that burns deep within the soul,
those tingling cells re-birthing so they never get old.
The love never gets old, the sex never routine,
the spiritually in tune always exist in between
in that place of the timeless, the knowing, the loving,
where the instinct survives whilst the heartbeat is throbbing.
Tantric love in its purest—
that is true living!
The ones on the wave inner peaceful yet shining;
utterly divining—harmonizing their minds in
the distortion of oneness which they've mastered through rhyming.
There's no need to feel bad and there's no use for shame
for all those who resonate get sparked all the same, and the
emotions and feelings that begin to unravel
emerge like flames on a wave telepathic.
And the emotions and feelings that begin to unravel
emerge like flames on a wave telepathic.

They have all the time they need, there's no need to rush,
Their patience, the turn on and both having mastered the art of love.
They please with passion—with tenderness and knowing,
with a mind that's all-seeing and techniques that are ultimate.
The tantric king and queen could last all night long,

keep on repeat the groove—their own song.
The tunes and the resonance that pulses through the speakers
allow them to both be the student and teacher.
They make love with their crown, they don't fuck with their root
but with heart and with soul, with greatness and truth;
from that place of ascension that knows how to make the other sing,
knowing exactly how to pleasure and how to do their own thing.
Their bodies flow in harmony, their minds harmonize as one,
tantric infusion with a lust that's pure love.
No separation between the mind and the self,
pure human ecstasy shining through in their sweat;
the rhyming and grinding through their bodies and sounds
allow their scene to never end and keep cycling around
allow their scene to never end and keep cycling around.

They have the master tune on replay until they reach climax,
their fusion, the heaven, and their orgasm, the transcendance.
They change Gaia's frequency through the intimacy they bring,
the soulful surrender that makes the other cells sing,
and when they are no longer merged they're still connected as one,
their own cells tingling with the other's pure love.
The spirituality in tune are awake from a dream,
the passion burns free whilst retaining their peace.
Primality and pulses become synchronized to the heart
where the mind is pure and free and time has no start—
no end or beginning, no desire to receive
the satisfaction that mortals may long to receive
for the spiritual is sexy simply from being,
it's as effortless to them as the fine art of breathing!
Their ethereal robe of beauty shines purely as divine
coming together in tantric fusion to blow the other's mind.

A Poetical Rendition

A magically oxygenated description,
a self-sustaining poetical rendition
of idea, rhyme and imagination—to serve;
the notion of breathing life into words.

It is word that gives life to our breath
for without language, we would get lost in the depth,
of the infinite sea of the unknown;
it is the sound of speech that swims us back home.

What would we be without verbal or written
communication which allows us to exist in—
this loving planet that gives breath to all life on our Earth?
Yet it is these spiralling spells creating the paradox that destroy our
     true worth.

Rationality, reason, word—they are illusion!
They teleport us back and forth in an eternal confusion
for when we think—we forget to feel—a lack of feeling distorting time
which all stems from an imbalance in the root of the mind.

These words provide a truth and a specific form of seeing
which can be perceived as contributing to our perceiving,
yet our body, mind and spirit are designed to work in harmony,
an overuse of brain-destroying our unity and connectivity.

Just like the mighty tree that begins as a seed
we can only heal our nature if we allow ourselves to breathe,
for these words are empty to the heartbeat of a tree,
yet without these energetic vibrations—
you and I would not be.

Now I have found my peace
as a seed will be planted and grow.
So, which came first—the tree, or the seed?
I guess only nature knows.

To Not Love Your Lover

To not love your lover
because of guilt, shame and self-blame.
To not love your lover because you feel so deeply,
a cosmic love triangle started from purity.

You can't escape your past—it's carried in your veins
so you rise up and stay strong,
just so you can keep singing your song.
Yet even stars rest in darkness.

A cosmic love triangle—but now the end of the affair,
she is made for the stage and shines everywhere—
cuts of her hair, her memories forgotten,
releasing all those locks of guilt and suppressions.

The crystal—she can't keep it any longer,
a former lover replaced with a best friend and lover;
but *to not love your lover?* Man, that's deep—
that's the true love that keeps a story bittersweet.

Majestic, connection, those moments of reflection
polluted with denial and self-loathing of her confession.
And she sees his new love and sees a girl clinging to a dream—
so desperately wants to be a queen but—feeds
off his light, a match made in heavens?

That's the karmic reward for her guilt and suppression.

Or is it the karmic projection of her former lover, a sadistic gift to
    his lifelong friends?
It all gets taken away in the end,
it all gets taken away—
in the end.

A cosmic love triangle made for the stage,
they are all stars—they all shine the same way,
and she hopes as she soars on by, they remember her spirit,
remember why she came here to win it—

because she loves, deeply.
And this is her melody,
her symphony—

and it's divine.

But she can no longer love lovers in that old age way,
she needs the magic, the mastery and the insane—
the type of mind that mortals call crazy,
the type of rhymes that non-divines see as maybes
as cynical, to her ways—
the type of minds that she'll come back to teach another day.

Another day,
in another way.

'That One'

She's the girl you see at the festival with crystals and fairy wings,
the crazy girl who dances and never ceases to sing.

She's the wild woman, the free spirit with the wacky colours,
the one who treats all with love, as family, sisters and brothers.

She is the priestess with the colourful clothes and feathers in her hair,
a drum in hand everywhere she goes, and some other instrument near.

She's 'that One.'

She's the silent one in the corner who knows how to hold space,
tarot cards and a clear mind, with a warm angelic face.

She's the one who's not afraid to get a little wild, to let her sexuality
    shine in all its sensuality,
the inner warrior burning bright in tantric superiority.

She's the girl who is not afraid to look you directly in the eye,
to gaze deep into your soul to seek the truth you hide.

She's the one who sees.

She is a queen—a true shamaness swirling round,
third eye activated to go round and connect the crowns.

She is the one who will ask you what star sign you are before asking
    your name,
sun sign, moon sign, life path and your favourite crystal coming first
    in the way she plays.

She is 'the One'—carefree and wild—who treats life as a game,
fun, joy and lightness of spirit with peace and love as her fame.

She is the kind one, the compassionate creature who will go up to a
    stranger in need,
offer some water, a blanket or food with a pure heart and absence of greed.

She is the one who will listen to you talk and offer perspectives that
    will blow your mind,
your life will be changed just from the ways she speaks—she sees
    from the divine.

She is magical—that crazy chick everyone knows at the end,
the lone wolf arriving solo and leaving with a community of friends.

She is a crystal.

She is a flower.

She is a priestess.

She is your spirit animal.

She is—

love.

The Duality of Language

The dissonance,
the resonance,
they separate me from you
whilst keeping us in tune.

The duality of existence,
unity through resistance;
polar opposites will attract at some point in time,
a connection maintained through the poetry of the mind.

We break the heart to mend it,
make the heart to break it;
we pain ourselves to find peace
whilst harmonising distortion for our release.

Our disparity allows us to entwine
whilst our communications create the divide,
this paradox of being forever continued through words;
the language of living with no purpose but to serve.

You say black so I say white,
you say day so I say night;
one says dark—so the other says light.
Our suffering is merely entertainment for language's delight.

Is there ever a wrong, ever a right?
Neither can claim victory over their own sight
as perceptions are just that—reflections of our own soul
so the disunity does us favour when we play out our notes' tones.

The sounds of surrender we long to hear exist only in a dream,
if only we could learn how to communicate in peace.
Perhaps if we listen, truly *listen* to the other's verse,
then we would hear the other's heartbeat
and there would be no need for words.

Immortal Destruction/ The Voice of the Ego

'Don't feel, you're not allowed,'
I told you to stop letting love seep through—go back to your denial.
Water down your emotions—repress what you cannot hide,
and don't step into greatness, continue in your lies.
'Don't feel I said', you must stay small and weak,
it's essential to dilute your greatness for a lesser reality.
Keep yourself stuck in mortality—continue in your cycle,
whatever you do, don't embrace your godly shining spiral.
Stop feeling, no! Go back under cover,
keeping playing to lust's temptation, do not love your lover.
Continue to drown your light away, continue to devolve,
smoke yourself into cells mortality, eat poisons and grow old;
keep on regressing all your wounds, your true feelings and your *soul*,
allow yourself to feel rejection so your story never gets old.
'No', I said—do not feel, you must keep running away,
yes, you've got—well done dear mortal—you're stuck inside my game.

You are mine—I've got you trapped inside my plot,
now the ego and darkness have you, your god particles start to rot.
Allow those memories of love and devotion to diminish into darkness,
forget all the celestial experiences and don't embrace your stardom.
That's it, my child, keep sipping on your poison,
lust for a vessel created in a hologram, crave eternal empty orgasms.
Feed off her, yes that's it, keep on getting your fix,
pour all your energy into your illusion so your purpose no longer exists.

Mmm, I feel so high knowing you keep on feeding me,
your lust and destruction, ego and darkness polluting real connectivity.
Your light is mine—it fuels desire, no more service to planet earth or others,
I will never let you leave this spiral so embrace your chosen darkness.

What's that—you think you have me fooled?
You truly think you have outsmarted me and that I'm the one confused?
No dear child—you are still trapped—the light you see is superficial,
you hide in—get lost in fact—a decision made in the artificial.
True love, true light, begins in something pure,
it grows from a seed and is nurtured over time, birthed directly from
    the source.
You can smile and believe you have managed to master me,
that I am just the ego and in fact, you have embraced your divinity;
but once again you would be wrong—you are still playing my game,
your vibration never truly transcended, your life never truly changed.
The life you lead was birthed from poison, a manipulated toxic atom,
a story created by my power which began in a seed of destruction.
I would say why don't you begin to feel, stop basking in your fake glory,
allow all real memories to shine through and start to remember the
    real story;
take a trip down memory lane and go straight back to the root
but no—don't—I won't allow it… how else would I keep you fooled?

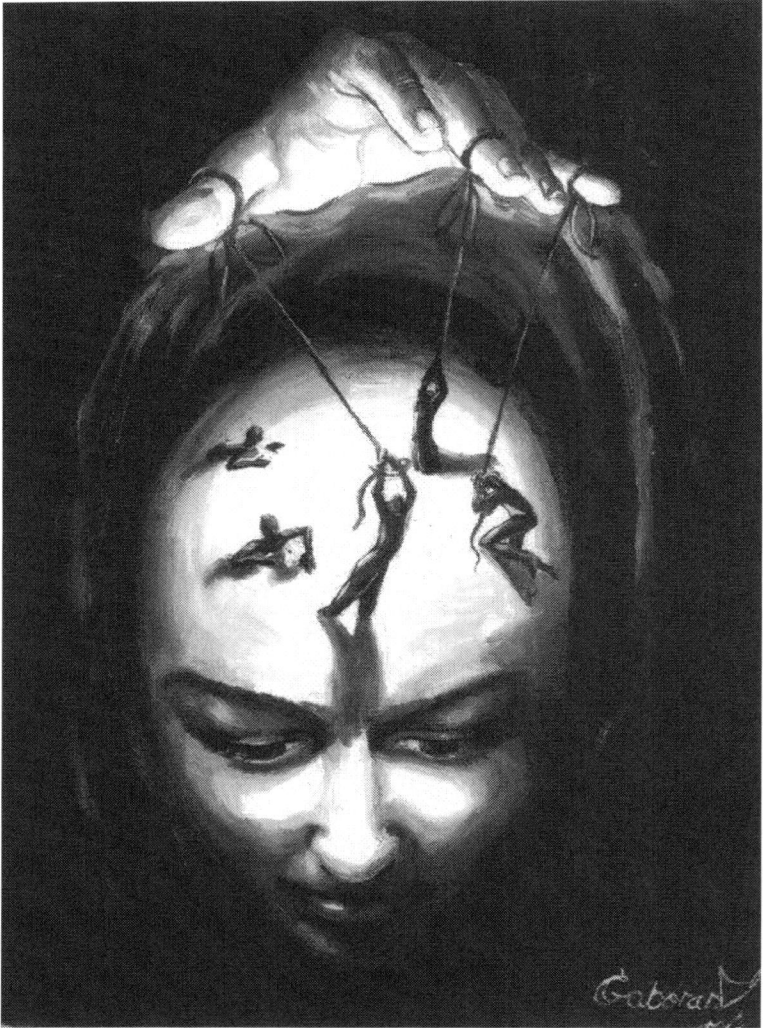

Mind Matters

He shot him,
just walked up to him in the street,
watched blood fly everywhere as he fell to his feet.
He searched his pockets for money,
smiling to himself.

How are these acts *funny?*

He thinks it's a joke—a game,
committing murder, robbing the dead
then walking carelessly away.

❀　❀　❀

She attacked her until she fell to the ground,
just ran up to this elderly woman and pounded her chest,
punched her repeatedly in the face then moved onto the next.
Anyone around her got brutally beat,
no remorse for the amount of blood flowing down the street.

❀　❀　❀

He parked up his overpowering truck next to a young local girl
and used his uniform and frightening presence to satisfy his urge.
He raped her—causing so much pain and hurt
he pulled her hair, forced her down, bruised her body and ripped her shirt.
He used and abused this girl, thinking he was free to do as he pleased…

She was only eighteen.

❀　❀　❀

They ran around with loaded guns
shooting innocent civilians whilst 'having fun.'

They believed they were winning this game they'd created,
lost in the world of violence and hatred.
Every day this is all they'd desire,
to become absorbed in the sounds of screams and gunfire.

When it was time to part ways,
moments between the murders went by in a daze
as their minds were numb with the knowledge that they would
    return to the screen;
hypnotized, lost in the game,
and magnetized to their seats.

Mind matters.

Hoponopono for Her Halo

He never saw her halo,
he just wanted to take and take,
he never saw her halo
he just laughed and called her fake;
a fraud, a charlatan—so many different names,
abuse, ridicule and slander were the way he played his game.

He never saw her halo—he was living in one dimension
purely from a physical world created with endless distractions.
He never felt the kindness, he never felt the heart,
a mind rooted in need and greed the only way he sensed from the start;
and all those beautiful qualities, the sacrifice and offering a helping hand
were instantly distorted with blurry vision polluted by the
    corruption of man.

The delusion, the confusion, the mind that says mine and yours
where the essence and qualities that make one human were
    sacrificed without remorse,
and the council of elders that stood around with judgmental eyes
    piercing down,
with so many illusions from mind's pollution continuously circling
    round—
could not destroy the humbleness and compassion that she breathed,
her lack of needing to prove herself to anyone providing her lasting peace.

He still never saw her halo—
he just wanted to take and take,
he never felt her halo
so he laughed and called her fake;
then he threw the stone aimed directly at her head,
harm was all he sought to cause, yet it fell effortlessly to the ground
    instead,
and the ripple he cast in her direction hit that universal wall,

the mirror projected his wish and intention, which inevitably made
    him fall;
for she is pure—she is real—she is not just the one dimension he is
and as his reflection, she became the shield, his lack of sight being
    key to his ignorance,
yet she tried to help him—still—she still tried to make him see
whilst his perpetual wish to destroy her halo kept him in purgatory.

And even as the flames were rising, spiralling around to burn
she stayed connected to her place of power, love being the strongest
    force and verb;
and they could not burn her, they could not cause harm, no matter
    how hard they tried
for her secret was compassion, an unbinding promise to keep
    healing, which all began inside
her mind.

For the final time, they cast the stone—this time with all their might,
they had attempted to shatter her beautiful halo so many different times.
She stayed strong, centred and connected to her light
and whispered the magic words: 'I love you, I'm sorry; you're right.'

Hoponopono.

The Voice of the Mystic

It is a lonely path
but happiness is a choice,
freedom is a choice.

It's a lonely path
yet I can choose to surround
with those I am blessed to have found,
and make me smile,
I can stay in company for a while.

Happiness is a choice,
love is my voice.
There is strength in solitude,
not meaning to sound rude
but I find comfort here,
in my own skin.

Now I manage a laugh
at the road of peace I see.
Perhaps no man nor husband nor marriage,
perhaps only solitude in a single golden carriage,
yet I feel blessed to walk the paths I choose,
divine angelic blessings sent out of the blue,
and many new ancient souls to meet on my journey,
remembering who we are and how we are never truly lonely.

It is a lonely path, this eternal life,
no man to surrender to as a devoted wife;
no body to hold as light fades to black,
and no entangled embrace as mortality shines back.
Sometimes curiosity comes when lying in my single bed
but then I feel my chest breathing;
heart beating,
and I feel peace instead.

Happiness is a choice.

I am never truly alone
for to be alone is to be *all one*,
until Earth's song is sung.
I guess I'll keep journeying through chosen paths,
when the seeds are fully grown, standing free as trees
and when we are no longer stealing honey from those hard-working bees;
when each child of Gaia recognizes their divinity,
remembers their connection to their Soul's timeless beauty.

When there is no war and we love unconditionally,
treat all we meet as members of our family.
Perhaps then my skin will feel the skin of another
and I will surrender fully to a husband and a partner.
Yet do I choose this path—
do I even have a choice?

My own inner voice leads me in other directions,
tells me to keep walking—seeing all as reflection
and not attaching to any creature for security as projection.

Please—do not mistake my solitary acceptance,
a part of self would love to share my essence on a deeper level,
and sometimes it is a lonely path

however, this mortal woman needs to be strong
remaining true to myself until my own song is sung.
Our Soul knows what is good for our growth
and which paths we must walk for the good of our Earth.

Love is a choice.

Life is forever fluid, perpetually changing,
timelines merging and simultaneously playing.

Perhaps I continue to fly with wings,
breathing deeply for my release,
choosing to remain my inner peace;

seeing all as light and love,
embracing my darkness within

and being *in love with love*.

It's a lonely road
yet my soul is free and soars above the sky,
looking down at the world I left and smiling from inside.
Knowing that each child of Gaia is fully free inside
and the path I chose was right in each moment,
as time is just the mind.

So now I embrace my mortal acceptance,
I am but a human creature with a body and emotions
yet I surrender and thrive in my own independence.
It is my motherly nature to look towards paths of family;
birthing the immortal light into my own mortality,
blessed to be surrounded by millions of siblings—
millions of mothers, fathers, distant relatives and children;
so many to love and share life with for eternity,
all here on mother earth as one global family.

It is a lonely path
yet I am blessed with my freedom—
with my heart,
with my purpose and my mind—
my spirit fully integrated into this body of mine.

And what is left to do but to accept we are one
and live life in devotion to Gaia's Earth song.

This is the Voice of the Mystic.

❊   ❊   ❊

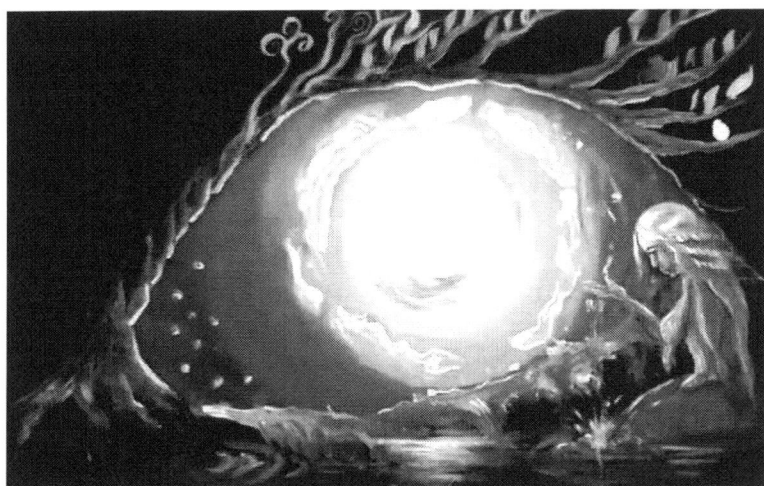

The Mystic & the Magician

The mystical woman,
she sees inside your soul,
seeking to help you grow.

Her powers enable her to intuitively know
using instinct with a witchy seeing,
subtlety changing the way you perceive things.

Silently, in solitude, protected in her aura
she feels *everything*, senses all be keeping to her peaceful inner
    demeanour.
This goddess appears to be just a girl
yet inside her skin, she is the creator of her world.

Like the old wise woman, she can tune into cosmic energies,
absorbing information from waking life and dreams.
Like the seer, she feels and sees everything as energy;
floating to whichever vibration calls to consciously affect your frequency.
She is magnetic beyond belief…
always on her radar
she can feel you regardless of how close or how far;
time and space matter not in her reality,
you are connected in a timeless quantum galaxy.
She can smell you—tune into your scent,
able to transcend the desires from the primal pulses sent.

Always showing understanding and compassion
she knows it is man's nature to turn towards destruction;
for her presence can be addictive,
stronger than any drug you've bore witness.

She captures you with her purity and unconditional love
stirring something inside your soul, a passion with each touch.
With each heartwarming smile and open affection,
each kind word and innocent submission;
for the mystic's veil has been lifted.

She lets you in but remains at ease being alone,
she can merge with your spirit yet knows her own soul is her home.
She loves you unconditionally and knows you deeper than any other—
this creature is a true Earth Mother;
the spirit of Gaia in human form,
she has made a promise and sworn
to protect her Earth and the realms you cannot see…
she lives full in her duty to serve and maintain her peace.

At times she appears odd,
rather crazy to the eye,
her mysterious ways may shock you or surprise;
she floats around as if on another dimension
with a calming aura,
free from all tension.

A magic fills the air…

A surreal feeling flowing, spinning and twisting;
is she from another world—
is she here just visiting?

The more you observe this magical creature
the more you start to see your true nature;
for she is a reflection; the aspect of yourself you hide,
she represents the purity and innocence which is usually denied.
And through all of your own and her own imperfections
she will only see you as pure light and perfection.
For she is the seer, the wise woman, the mystic and the healer,
she is always dreaming, always learning, and being a humble teacher.

She digs deeper to seek what you hide
with no fear to get lost in your eyes,
trying to seek the vibration that will help you evolve
choosing to see only the best and guiding you home.
This woman knows every being has their own blueprint;
a frequency so unique that it is still hidden deep within.

So she pulls it out of your being.

She plants the seed
then gives you space, time to breathe—
then leaves;
she goes her own way
reminding you nothing is here to stay,
except you.

You are the only one who can live up to your destiny—
the seer in her sees the power in you and tries to help you see.
Yet when she returns from her absence, always changed,
for she has left this world over and over whilst you repeat the same
    cycles every day;
if she sees you are stuck in your ways
making no attempt to change—same story every day?
She will simply let you be.
The travelling mystic wants you to be the change you wish to see
but only you can grow that tree;
she just made aware of the seed.

Her presence reminds you of your own greatness
her light glows from creator to creator.
Although she will only ever show you love,
help your soul soar high above;
do not fall mortally in love with this magical creature.
Everyone wants the magic; the beauty, the essence,
but with the mystery comes absence, detachment, and independence.

She will show you divinity, she will show you passion;
the mystical lover will take you to realms and dimensions
that you thought only existed in a fairytale...
You will be magnetised to the depths of her spirit and love,
you will entwine through eternity and feel *true* love.

She will show you how to breathe, truly breathe as the god you are,
and all illusions will fade to nothing until you remember your crown;
she will guide you and heal you whilst your imprisoned walls
    crumble down.
The amnesia cocoon you created will cease to exist,
the king you have always been will shine freely in bliss;
the mystical woman will bring you back to the depths of your soul,
she will heal and surrender to you until you return home.

Once you are enticed by her magical ways
and once you have remembered—awake from the maze,
she will leave.
It will pain her deeply, but she will go,
both of you free for your next cycle of growth.
A travelling soul,
lost—yet home
living fully in her duty to protect and serve,
she is just a passerby here on Earth.
Some say she is from another world...
Yes dear Magician, she will love you—
yet she came here alone.

Could you fall in love with this divine creature knowing it could end;
the pain that comes with surrendering to a lover and best friend?
The Mystic and the Magician are meant to entwine as one heart,
yet destiny makes sure they float freely away, at the end and from the
    start.

❋   ❋   ❋

The warrior of light,
he makes her feel alive;
igniting a passion deep inside.
He commands her respect and admiration;
usually feeling no tension
the mystical woman—powerful and present,
becomes lost to the magician's eyes,
increasing his presence.

A vulnerability begins to take hold...

The more she decreases her boundaries and merges with his energy,
the more she feels protected and free to just *be!*
This usually independent and powerful creature
is playing the student, no longer the teacher.
She learns the true meaning of being an equal and a peer,
yet she feels fear.

His tender touch makes her grow weak,
and his powerful aura reminds her she seeks
a companion, a lover, a soul to merge with—
someone to share her magical world with.
The feeling of surrender to love with another
allows her light to grow stronger and gives sense to her wonder.
For the mystic loves magic, the unknown and surprise,
exactly what she sees when gazing into the magician's hypnotic eyes.
Yet, like a true warrior of light, he has his own path
but now she has bonded, merged into the dark;
and the safety she felt when held, skin to skin,
disappears as magically as the moments begin
for the warrior's love is a drug like no other,
he reminds her how to be a sensual earth mother.

Once she has him deep within her soul,
the warrior will move onto the next goddess seeking growth;
for he is a traveller; independent and free,
here to show the mystical woman she is on her own journey.

Could she give herself fully to this divine creature knowing it could end;
the pain that comes with surrendering to a lover and best friend?
The Mystic and the Magician are meant to entwine as one heart,
yet destiny makes sure they float freely away at the end and from the start.

Destiny makes sure they float freely away

  at the end,

   and from the start.

❀ ❀ ❀

Haikuvolution

The old ancient oak
patiently waiting for light,
still in night's dark cloak.

The wise owl, unique
existing in the unknown—
mind thrives in mystery.

The subtle echoes
from moonlight's sensual laugh,
yet silent in throne.

❁   ❁   ❁

Patient dear earthworm,
slow and steady while you seek—
the bird is hungry.

An air so loving
seduced into temptation,
imprisoned yet free.

Beast and beauty: One,
the eagle's gifts soar tonight,
art and murder sung.

Beast and beauty: One,
the eagle's gifts soar tonight,
art and murder sung.

Range Master

One timeline,
two timeline—three;
monogamy, polygamy, celibacy?

Past lives, present lives; future lives—
which ones are true and which ones are lies?
Can you really, truly love two people simultaneously,
completely, authentically and wholly?

You are a human yo-yo!
You're a range master within with different frequencies, you know.
Your self wants this route, doesn't want that,
then your different self doesn't want it and wants to go back.

The human dilemma—so many timelines,
which one do you align to with so many minds?
Do you want to be in your root, playing from your sacral,
or would you rather be in your crown and choosing a life that's magical?

One timeline,
two timeline; three—
we are merely a range of frequencies.
Which one is true, which one is real…
how are we supposed to know when they all feel right?

Or is your energy body dis-aligned?
Higher self—heart—spirit and soul—
these are the ones I feel, you know.
Yet the others still exist, the others are still real—
what's your best life—what makes you feel
your soul?

No—not others' motives and needs—*your* soul,
or are you getting pulled into another's flow?
Do you even know anymore?
Do you even know?

Check Mate / Lessons in Love

The goddess glided to her door
and opened it up with a welcome warm,
she had laid out flowers to match the young soul's colours,
taking note of all things honest.

Red for fire, courage and passion,
a colour mars himself would desire with attraction;
orange and yellow for expression and boldness
yet spiritually young in an ancient cycle of oldness.

Weeks went by and she observed a pattern,
her once own love was in constant distraction,
failing to see the old soul's needs
he lay each night beside his queen.

So this young woman packed up all her possessions,
suggested that they swap with pure intentions.
She gave up her humble abode which she had spent years working for
and once again opened up her door.

This sensitive soul had spent years in sacrifice,
years in sheer commitment, dedicated her life—
to helping others, engaged in service;
nothing too much for a heart so earnest.

Months went by with sharing freely,
she literally gave her life—*completely*;
all her goals, rewards and dreams
she gave up in the name of love to this young new queen.

Then it came to the final cycle,
just one week until things returned to their natural alignment;
she was set to have her sanctuary back,
her humble home and life on track.

But leaving gracefully was too much for a girl ruled by war
and the power of Mars came through in full force.
Everything that was honest, pure and selfless
was turned into a reality, nasty and selfish.

She destroyed the nature of a plant—she had simply made a mistake,
she then took and left in the most unnatural way.
She had misheard an offering given in kindness,
and in her self-rage, truth was turned into blindness.

She shouted, she cursed, she criticised and spoke badly,
she turned love and beauty into something pure ugly.
Her warpath twisted the most selfless reality
into one of destruction, distortion and brutality.

But cycles went by without a word
and the young woman had returned to her divine world;
she wrote words of beauty, she planted new seeds,
she remained content in her world of found peace.

This Old Soul Queen truly was living in gold—
each choice she made for the good of the whole.
Kindness, genuineness and heart defined her,
no sacrifice too much to make another's life less hard.

Her last comfort that gave her peace,
her final blessing for giving up the rest of her needs,
was an instrument of beauty, brown like the earth—
a tool for the shaman to the spiritual world.

She would play songs of truth, she would vibrate out notes of grace,
she would bring peace and joy to her neighbourhood each day.
This beauty was used as a tool for pure healing,
in selflessness and service, *rooted* in feeling.

Then one day Check Mate arrived,
all things divine had been alchemized into lies,
the light of the music and the vibration of service
were transmuted into evil birthed from jealousy and darkness.

But at that moment the Old Soul realized she had won,
Check Mate had come as the gift of no love
and everything she had done, the life she had given away
was alchemized into gold the moment they tried to take her song away.

For she sees the energy behind every action,
she has transcended all of the physical distractions;
she sees from a world that's multi-dimensional,
and knew that the experience was significant—biblical.

That tool that now sits unused daily without magic
was the last chord holding her to a world that was tragic;
a world where she gave up her life to someone else
and only received judgement, abuse and offense.

The cheating move of trying to take her King
inevitably made the real Queen win,
as the goddess who opened her door with open arms despite giving
    all her dreams away
was then allowed her to make her final move, in love, in truth—

Check Mate.

Time Is an Atom

Life is just cycles—consciousness vast,
stories are just frequencies waiting to be cast;
our cells hold the coding, our spirit holds the key,
through our hearts we can activate yet our eye must still see.
Individual and collective are one and the same—
we came here with a seeded story; we came to change the game;
just like a snake sleeping DNA can remain dormant
but when we finally awaken that prelude, it will be our final performance.

Life is just cycles—consciousness vast,
stories are just frequencies waiting to be cast;
our cells hold the coding, our spirit holds the key,
we didn't come all the way to planet earth to not fulfill destiny—
rememory.

❊   ❊   ❊

Silence is only illusion of her depth...

Time is an atom.

Crystal Traveller

She's flying—high,
looking down at the world she left and smiles—
all the pain and darkness slowly begin to fade
and memories of sweet music take her back to a brighter day.

She's soaring—high above the clouds,
heaven is on her side and her mind no longer circling round.
She's left the spiral, she's floated through the gap,
escaped the beliefs and oppressions that were toxically holding her back.

She really is flying, existing on another plane,
looking down at her mortal friends who she knows she will see
    another day,
and they are smiling back at her, knowing she is completely free,
although they have chosen different parts they love each other
    unconditionally.

And the thought of mortality and returning back starts to make her drop,
looking up at the heavens and flying among the gods.
She sees the mountain, she has her chance, if only she could reach
    out her hand,
all she has to do is lose all fear, be transported to another land.

She is flying among the stars, celestial angels by her side,
surrounded by eagles, golden lights, and crystals floating in between
    the skies.
And even in this euphoric bliss, the top where many mortals cannot
    reach,
her cells begin to tingle, her immortality starts to speak.

She is alone, she gave up her one true love,
she knows it, she feels it—she sees the whole story—she gave up
    love, for what?
For fame, recognition, for success and enlightenment,
for the desire to do what most humans don't and be part of the holy
    establishment.

The gods all around her smile that special smile
for they know she has finally harmonized her mind.
They all start laughing—not evil—but pure,
her full embrace a spark to keep them laughing more.
She is in a circle being judged compassionately by the gods,
she is pure vision, astrally activated with her soul's plan pouring
    through in force.
Yet she is stuck—she knows what she must do—but she can't,
she knows she needs to return to earth, find her flame and hold out
    her hand.
She wants to help him—so desperately—there is nothing more she
    desires than to lift him up,
to hold out her hand, give him her heart, and surrender to the plot.
For she knows the cycle he is in is karmic, a choice she made him make,
the story he kept on returning to take away his pain.

She really is at the top of the mountain—there is no higher height
    to reach,
each time she gets to this space it all comes back to the same story.
So she centres herself, puts on her brave face and gets helped back
    down to earth,
the celestials and the angels assisting her down the stairs.
They will forever help her—here to serve her in every now,
her devotion a golden ticket to be taken care of all around the world.

Yet before she takes her final step into the great unknown
she asks them that one question she's asked many times before.
They smile that same smile, this time more gently, and without the
    need for words
for she has been in this same place time after time, the same
    response in different worlds.

They don't even have to answer, she feels the truth tingling through
    her core,
she smiles that knowing smile and embraces the journey ahead once
    more.
She thanks them for their guidance, she stays connected to their love,
puts on her celestial backpack and floats contently back to earth.
She will keep her story with her for the rest of her days, hold the
    answer strong within her heart,
remembering once again she has travelled long and far.
She smiles down at her future whilst smiling up at her celestial family,
holding the crystal around her heart strongly with truth and clarity.
She's walking on a golden path with eternal abundance and heavenly
    contact as her guide,
she always has access to the other worlds and unseen forces by her side.
She carries the vibration and maintains the energy wherever she
    freely goes,
knowing that at any stage she wishes, she is free to return back home.

It's easy now—this was her final contact,
she's been there many times before but always went back to black.
But the truth remains inside her cells—she carries it as her pride,
she journeyed inside to the core of her soul's cell where destiny
    cannot hide.
And every particle, every epiphany, every element of her entire existence
is clear as the tears she will no longer produce, as clear as
that special crystal.
Her smile her gift, her strength her blessing, and her soul her very guide,
she now travels around the world in Gold, pure love for the rest of
    her life.

There is space for another on her magical ride.

A Swan Song of Gold

The drum roll beats and the stage is set—
she feels the pounding in her chest.
The invisible is finally about to be shown,
a behind the scenes world only the director knows.

She's been waiting a lifetime—shaping a masterpiece,
silently creating a new world from dreams.
Those who don't believe in magic are about to be shown
for the next act is breathtaking… a Swan Song of Gold.

Soul Sex

Sensations; vibrations, rhythmic temptations
spirit in the flesh of two divine creations.

When two atoms collide, space and time
melt into an eternal dance,
pure human ecstasy fuelling their trance.

Shiva and Shakti, a dance of dual vibrations,
god and goddess, the yin and yang of creation.
Queen and King, two conscious beings in their Crown,
love as Source infinity spiralling round.

They are from the stars,
beautiful lights from different worlds
their hearts merging into one through connection of soul.

Soul sex at its purest, lust and passion prime,
true love in epiphany, no illusion from divine.

Chemistry, kinetic energy,
primality and higher self free,
a merging of all minds for true harmony.

When galaxies come together in an energetic dance like this,
through the heart ache, the heart break—when they merge back
    into the abyss,
this Shiva and shakti know they are forever entwined,
their souls connected and their story sublime.

History and herstory, past lives and future
knowing they have both been the student and the teacher.
Memory contained in both the teardrop and the sweat,
for making love like this is more than just sex, it's *soul sex*.

Tribe's Wombman

Many do not understand how she can simply be—
be pure, be real—be love, be sexual, be spiritual and be free.

For she sees—she is multidimensional, a holographic drop of
    consciousness;
she has embraced it all and aims to evolve through all her knowledge.

She is ancient—she knows she has shared lives with many,
all her connections in this life transcend all states of duality.

She knows she is a lover, a goddess in human form,
and she knows how to keep it real and when to keep it pure.

She is a tribeswoman, the mother, sister, friend and lover,
she is the magician, the king, the god and the warrior.

She knows her relation-ships transcend the mortal,
that there are so many vibrations and frequencies in one story.

She is both masculine and feminine, man and woman—
she is a Tribe's Wombman.

She is a Tribe's Wombman.

Grace Note

We are the masters, the magicians of music,
combining notes, tones and melodies,
harmonizing subtle sounds for our remedies.

We are the magic makers, the heartbeat—the groove,
vibrating out as sound to move us all in tune.

Some say we're educators, aliens in disguise sent from the heavens
    above,
others say we are students rhythmically learning through an infinite
    sea of love.
It is our Mother, our earth, that allows us to sing as one,
differing notes combining, allowing for Gaia's song to be sung.
Our ancestors reminding us to remember, re-member,
forgotten dreams here to be seen
recognized through these intimate channels of frequency.

We are the shamans, the healers—the mystical music weavers
existing simultaneously in multiple realities,
being present now to restore unity to duality;
our telepathy allowing for our minds to entwine as one,
a sensual seduction of heart and soul, so pure, so real—begun.

Now you see, it has always been,
me and you, this destiny.
These golden wings hidden for thousands of years,
the magic of mastery polluted through darkness, desire… fear.

Now we rise—now we shine,
the distortion of our sound dissipating back to the infinite where it
    arose.
Where you and I were no separate, same source, different notes.
What is the purpose of language when we feel what's real and true?
Love—true love—this melody, this groove.

Love is unconditional, mystical and poetic,
it requires no explanation yet we use language to convey it.
These spiralling spells echo from the ether so we can communicate
    in verse,
these words—vibrations,
energetic manifestations
of the heart and the feeling;
the only thing that is real in
this twisting and spiralling reality of illusion—
magical and miraculous with no more confusion.
Ancient eyes and human disguise with no more denial to the purity
    we seek,
for the truth is, we all long to be free...

So let us rise and harmonise,
let us all play out our notes
and return to the eternal sea of oneness
where there is no need for words.

Now our song is heard.

✿   ✿   ✿

Acknowledgements

We all win and lose, and we all have a light and a shadow. This book is for all who have loved me and I have loved; for Gaia—our beautiful planet, and her health and harmony, and, most importantly, for myself.

Self love and respect is the way.

About the Artist

Alina Gaboran is a visual artist for whom the creative process is an act of bearing witness to and capturing the emerging facets of the Self. These facets are a mirror reflecting both the artist's soul and the collective conscious energy field. Alina's journey through painting maps a transper-sonal search for answers and inspiration in the human body, nature, and their interconnection. She believes art is the most beautiful way to become whole; it is a bridge between the material and inner worlds and a way of discovering the mysteries of the human psyche.

Alina explores themes of the human psyche, the sacred feminine, soul metamorphosis, death and rebirth, life cycles, and balance and healing and has been inspired by Jungian psychology, art therapy, transper-sonal psychology, visionary art and mindfulness. She has exhibited in Romania, Ireland and the UK and has had her art featured in a number of magazines, galleries and community art festivals.

Through her own personal healing experiences in the healing and evolu- tionary power of art, Alina explores the art's curative potential supporting others through her passion as a visual artist. She is currently training to become an art therapist.

Contact Alina:

alina.gaboran@yahoo.com

www.facebook.com/alinagaboran.art

About the Author

Grace Gabriella Puskas is a teacher. She believes fully that we can transcend lower vibrational ways of being into a higher and evolved state connected to frequencies of love, compassion and universal healing.

Being both a Reiki Master teacher & shaman and musician, poet and lyricist, Grace sees all of life itself as frequency and vibration; as music. She has entered both the darkest and lightest places of her soul and is on a lifelong journey of truth, aware that anything she experiences on an individual level is reflective of the uni-versal story in play and can, there- fore, be used for healing and collective evolution. She has full intentions to restore wholeness and healing to herself and others through the use of crystals, sound, holistic linguistics, poetry, music, energy healing and herbal medicine, and is a qualified and naturally experienced Reiki Master teacher, shamanic energy healer, dream interpreter, medicinal herbalist, crystal healer and qi gongist; in addi-tion to having experienced a very real shamanic death and rebirth initiation in 2012.

Grace's debut book, *A Message from Source*, was a result of winning the national Local Legend Spiritual Writing Competition, the blue-print poem first being channelled in 2012. It was this first collection of 33 poems that inspired her to create *A Story of One: Transcen-dance*. Her life's philosophy is entwined with her beliefs and faith in music being the one thing that can change the world and bring us all together. It was her deep love and respect for nature, the musical universe we live in, and staying integrally committed to aligning with her higher self and evolution that set her out on her journey as a teacher and way shower for others. She believes it is through ancient tantric practices of achieving higher states of consciousness and evolving to our highest potential through a form of 'tantric transcen-dence'—a unification of mind, heart and spirit into a state of pure unconditional love—that true healing and unity can be restored to Gaia and the collective consciousness energy field.

Although it is her shamanic roots that is the basis of her motivations she has been greatly inspired by musicians such as Victor Wooten (*One*), Esperanza Spalding (*Unconditional Love*), and Bob Marley (*One' Love*) therefore uses sound, music and poetry to shift frequencies in self and in others for best possible realities and timelines.

In 2016, Grace Gabriella Puskas was invited into the UK's Top Leading Evolutionaries on a public vote by the global heart centred media platform, Source.tv, recognized for her contributions to the global shift in consciousness. Grace is currently writing her third and final collection of poetry, *Earth Print*, which is a complete work of poetic blueprints for the natural world including spirit animals, star signs and planets, goddess archetypes and spiritual deities, and special gems and natural herbs.

Grace's only wish is to assist in the restoring of unity to planet earth and the evolution of humanity's consciousness, living out her true musical vibration as unconditional love.

Contact Grace:

You can contact grace at gracegabriella33@gmail.com

Celestial Poetry, her free poetry blog, can be seen here:
www.celestialpoetry.co.uk

Her personal website is www.gracegabriellaunlimited.com

End Note / Alternate Timeline
Her Letter to Her (future) Lover

I'm sorry it's taken me so long to do this,
but the truth is—I love my independence!
I thrive in free-spiritedness and have made going solo look like a
    masterpiece,
yet I am not a masterpiece: I am art.
I am straight lines, and the bent and curvy ones.
I am dark and dreamy like the moon yet blinding like the sun.
I am all the colours, the shadow and the clear canvas.
I have got so used to being alone that I have become complete
    within myself,
needing no man to complete me.

Yet you make me vulnerable.
You are the only man who makes me feel weak,
the one I become excited around and who does make me complete
because you motivate me to be the best me I can be.
Just knowing you are in my life makes me want to master myself,
master my mind and emotions; master my spirit and body and
    evolve into the true goddess that I am.
We are not mortals—we are destined for greatness.
I know of your godliness and you know of my magic,
I know I can be too much, I know I can push us too far sometimes,
yet you also know my motivations behind the madness.
You see how I see—your eye knows my eye,
I can seduce you entirely just through my rhyme;
this ecstasy that we feel is completely telepathic,
the feeling your feeling proving my magic.

Yet you're still scared?
My soul is screaming for you to embrace me yet you succumb
    to the fear?

Why do you think it has taken us so long to come together in the
    physical,
if our love is only a fantasy—a fairy tale illusion,
our mind and emotions linger in the ether until we embrace the
    inevitable fusion.
Yet my intensity and fire make you question yourself?
You know I am the real deal so you deny yourself?
Why?

I am speaking directly to you yet you still choose the fear,
is it because you know that my love is eternal and real?
I'm literally having a conversation with you throughout time and space,
our energy bodies dancing, freely.

Are we worthy for such love, or are we still plagued by our fears,
will we let insecurity and a fear of rejection dilute what we feel?
Are we ready?

I'm sure you energetically asked me this once,
and I replied, 'I'm never ready.'

That was a lie.

I have always been ready because I have always been complete,
so if you can accept that I am already a masterpiece
you can be my colour, my shading and the canvas—
I invite you to share in my spirit and madness!
You have been waiting patiently, and I'm sorry for my delay
I guess I have gotten so used to going solo in this game.
Together we can rise to the highest of heights,
the divine godly gifts combined in superhuman delight.

Just, please, don't try to control me, possess or suppress,
the fear of suppression or preventing my best
is what will make me say 'I'm never ready.'
Jealousy, possession, dominating control—
these don't work for me,
I'm looking for the real deal—the source as duality.
I want you to be complete and content when alone,

I want you to connect and have fun when I'm at home;
when I'm doing my own thing, connecting with others—
this is the only way it will work.
I will be exclusive to you yet I need my independence.
I need to be free and have a healthy balance
and I promise you, I will not leave you.
I've had many lovers yet this love is deep,
this is the kind that you know you must keep.

I know how hurt we have been my love, we both have deep wounds
    and pain.
Our eye is both a curse and a blessing,
'nothing is forever' yet our love is eternal.
We know what it's like to have loved and to have lost,
to have given our all and to have had broken our trust.
We have both loved others, many, in this life and others,
yet I trust you,
I love you,
I'm ready to embrace you!
I'm ready to surrender to you and only you.

My love...
we have journeyed together throughout all time and space,
we recognize the other through our eyes and souls gaze.
Your energy is addictive—my cells tingle and come to life,
your aura a natural drug which makes me feel high.
When I try to suppress how I feel about you, my life becomes dull,
    depressed,
untrue—
I feel like I'm living a lie without surrendering to you.

Yet I am dual in nature and long to be free.

So here is my truth:
the only reason it has taken me so long to do this is due to my need
    for detachment,
the need to feel free and soulfully independent.
Yes, you are the only man I can share my love with,
allowing the fire and passion to be free in pure bliss.

The ancient priestess in me longs to be free,
angelic submission for tantric release.
Yet you cannot tie me down (metaphorically, you can literally)
you can do things to me that no other could,
I am open to you...
I will be your angel and I will be your priestess,
I will submit and succumb to you on all dimensions.

This is the beauty of our connection,
you see me for who I am.
You know of my beauty and divinity, my purity and innocence;
yet you know of my wildness and my animal essence.
Two lone wolves; two crazy dreamers,
unique and misunderstood yet together—we're fearless.

It's time to get real—no more illusion,
the fantasy can be grounded with no more confusion,
my invitation is here and I'm waiting for you;
let's take it to the next level—
you know what to do.

Grace's Story

Seven Years ago I set out on a quest, a quest to see what heights I
could reach,
I absorbed ancient wisdom, endless knowledge, and immersed
myself in study.
I enrolled in a selection of therapies that I believed were to be of help
for humanity, the animals, nature and the ecosystems; the one unity
that is planet earth.

I gave up every poison that ever polluted my system,
alcohol, drugs in all their connotations, and substance that lead to
mind's confusion.
Whilst others around me partied, I became the hermit,
sat in my room to push my mind, my soul and my being to their
limits.

Meditation became my drug, compassion became my mantra,
Purity, gentleness, kindness and grace were the qualities that pushed
me further.
Every day and every night I became obsessed to be the best version
of me,
seeking humbleness, stillness and depth to replace all feelings of
negativity.
Greed, pettiness, envy and blame—
competition, comparison, recognition and fame;
anger, judgement, intolerance and spite
literally dissipated from daily life.

The quest I set out was a road less travelled,
the mind I created forged from Source, physical matter created from
spiritual atoms.
The way I perceive from my silence and quiet was a quest I began
from the heart,
knowing within that no matter what happened love would be the
end and start.

Love became my only mantra, my only wish for humanity and our
    world,
and all the illusions that once existed no longer had a space in my soul.
Yet on my journey into pure surrender, pure trust in my inner voice
    and higher self
I began to remember I had a real purpose, a reason for my passion
    to transcend
the physical distractions—the greed, the envy and hate,
those things that kept you in a state of suffering, of offence,
    judgement and blame.
For these don't exist in my world, a world where you lead by soul,
a world where you can sense things yet to come, use senses outside
    the physical world—
because you know.

Interconnection became my reality,
a world rooted in oneness replaced duality;
kindness, giving, service and love
were the new found ways of being to replace human grudge.
Need, want and endless pursuit
no longer had space when living from Crown and root,
and in my sacrifice to give myself to the plan spirit wanted
I found myself absorbed into a life and world enchanted.

Now I sit and look around, grounded in what I have created—
endless years of sacrifice, strength and sheer courage,
with a beautiful home as an early inheritance gifted my beloved
family because they know that whilst everyone else was partying I
    was engaged in study—
in bettering myself, in striving for perfection, in placing my career
    and service first,
my sense of devotion, duty and responsibility giving me the gift of
    trust.

A new path manifested where my passion is my career,
devotion to my Soul's goals and dreams making physical life become
    crystal clear
and my chosen service—helping others through healing and the
    written word

allowed me to be welcomed to so many places, in the UK and
   around the world.
When we act from service, a desire to put other's needs above our own,
the universe gives us the gifts we need to make earth our one true
   home.
Love and respect for planet earth, the animals, plants and nature itself
is the only way we can see our lives thrive and stop living in fear and
   regret.
Once we realize we are one, all brothers and sisters here to stay
we will treat everyone as if they are our own extended family
   member here in the same game.

Every action yields a ripple and every word or thought a consequence,
what we put out we will receive, your wish or intention your own
   enchantment.
We are all mirrors here and we are here to live out best life,
what you wish on others will come back, the law of attraction
   matching your vibe.

So live from soul! Live from heart—remember that there is a higher
   law,
it is never too late to follow your dreams, break the mould and
   create your own path.

It all starts with the heart.

Printed in Great Britain
by Amazon